This book belongs to:

____

____

____

Alfie was a lively and healthy little girl who lived in a big city with his family.

The blocks of offices, flats and apartments in the city were so tall and from the windows you could look out and see for miles into the distance.

At night the lights from the tall buildings twinkled brightly. At sunrise a beautiful golden glow shone reflected from the glass windows all around!

3

Alfie's grandparents were both from the beautiful Caribbean island of Jamaica, known for its high mountains, beautiful beaches and musically talented people.

They travelled from the tropical paradise - where fruit and vegetables grew in abundance, to work in England in the 1950's.

England was cold with grey skies when they disembarked the ship with so many other enthusiastic young people from the Caribbean.

PEGRAMS

They rented a small room in the City
close to the hospital where they were
able to get jobs. His Mum was a nurse
and his Dad was an engineer.

Alfie was the fourth child of five, he had three brothers and one sister. Alfie would enjoy playing with his siblings inside the hallways and out in the garden of their home.

It was so much fun! They dressed up, sang joyful songs and acted in short plays they had created with other children in the neighbourhood.

Alfie loved school and his hand would often shoot in the air to answer the teacher's questions.

His eyes would sparkle as he waited to hear his name called out and he usually got the correct answers!

15

Alfie was very confident and was quite strong for his age. He could run very fast and would often win races at school against other children in his year.

Alfie strived for excellence in secondary school. He would read his books and always did his homework neatly and on time.

His teachers were very happy with the homework he handed in. He would always get marks of 9 out of 10 or 10 out of 10!

When his teachers were happy, Alfie was happy!

Alfie thought for a long time about what he
should do when he was grown up.

His teachers told him he should go to university
because he had so much potential!

Alfie realised that some children in his school were not always brushing their teeth as they should. Eating sugary food meant that sometimes their teeth had small holes or cavities which could painful!

He saw that in older people, teeth could become wobbly and break especially if they had not looked after their teeth when they were young.

Alfie wanted to help others to look
after their teeth and keep them
straight and clean.

He decided that he wanted to
study to become a dentist and an
orthodontist. He had always liked
to brush his own teeth, keeping
them clean and giving his a
brilliant smile.

At first the teachers were not very sure that he was able to do all of the hard work that was needed to become a dentist.

However, Alfie made sure that he applied to a dental school and worked hard to get the necessary Advanced-level grades in his school subjects!

When Alfie was 17, he received the news that the had achieved the grades he needed! He had to decide whether he wanted go to work or leave his family to go to university.

There were plenty of jobs available and he could have gone to work in a bank or in an office. Certainly, the money he would earn from a job could be given to his Mummy and Daddy so they could use it to buy clothes and food for the large family.

On the other hand, he enjoyed learning and really wanted to study more. He wanted to become a dentist!

BANK

He was so happy to start the course which took four years to complete. There was lots of time spent in the classroom and looking into patients' mouths to make sure their teeth and gums were healthy.

At dental school, Alfie learned how to deal with cavities, infections and how to take out bad teeth.

He encouraged patients to eat healthily, brush their teeth using the correct techniques and good quality toothpaste.

He wanted to make sure that the enamel, dentine and the gums were protected from decay and disease.

With good teeth, patients are able to smile nicely and chew their food to digest it properly!

Once Alfie completed dental school, he became a dentist for few years before going back to University and completing a Masters degree - to become an orthodontist. He did very well!

This meant that he would specialise in straightening crooked teeth, both in children and in adults so that they could have a nice smile.

35

Alfie always does excellent work for his patients.
They are always very happy with the results of nice
straight teeth and lovely smile!

They can smile and be confident with their
family, school friends, work colleagues and
customers.

37

Alfie has become a dedicated dentist and orthodontist. He enjoys helping people have healthy and straight teeth.

Maybe you could become a dentist or orthodontist one day, just like his!

If you want to be a dedicated dentist and, take a look at these references to learn how!

<u>For Kids:</u>

Kids Britannica
Kids Britannica page on dentistry.
https://kids.britannica.com/kids/article/dentist/611077

Kiddle
Kiddle encyclopedia page on dentistry.
https://kids.kiddle.co/Dentistry

BBC bitesize
BBC bitesize page on teeth.
https://www.bbc.co.uk/bitesize/topics/z7x78xs/articles/zsp76yc

Weebly
GCSE page on teeth and tooth decay.

https://biology-igcse.weebly.com/human-teeth-and-dental-decay.html

For parents and guardians:

UCAS
UCAS website for studying dentistry in the UK.
https://www.ucas.com/explore/subjects/dentistry

University Expert
University Expert page on helping your child get into dentistry.
https://universityexpert.co.uk/how-to-help-your-child-get-into-dentistry/

Wellsmile
Information page on the dental specialty of orthodontics.
https://www.wellsmile.co.uk/schools/career-in-orthodontics/

Colgate
Career pathway to becoming an orthodontist.
https://www.colgate.com/en-us/oral-health/adult-orthodontics/how-to-

become-an-orthodontist

What do you want to be when you grow up? Draw it
below!

Notes!

Check out some other books in the series!

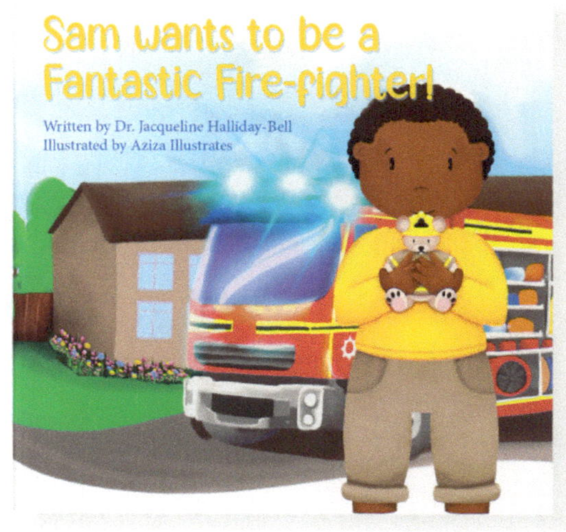

www.ingramcontent.com/pod-product-compliance
Lightning Source LLC
Chambersburg PA
CBHW042123030726
47599CB00002B/321

9 781917 162142